4.

chicago:

city

on the

make

BY

NELSON ALGREN

CHICAGO: CITY ON THE MAKE

THE MAN WITH THE GOLDEN ARM

SOMEBODY IN BOOTS

NEVER COME MORNING

THE NEON WILDERNESS

DOUBLEDAY & COMPANY, INC.

chicago:

city

on the

make

by

Nelson

Algren

GARDEN CITY, NEW YORK, 1951

This book is based on an article
first published in *Holiday* magazine.

With heart at rest I climbed the citadel's
Steep height, and saw the city as from a tower,
Hospital, brothel, prison, and such hells,
Where evil comes up softly like a flower . . .

Whether thou sleep, with heavy vapors full,
Sodden with day, or, new appareled, stand
In gold-laced veils of evening beautiful,

I love thee, infamous city!

—Baudelaire

one

the
hustlers

To the east were the moving waters as far as eye could follow. To the west a sea of grass as far as wind might reach.

Waters restlessly, with every motion, slipping out of used colors for new. So that each fresh wind off the lake washed the prairie grasses with used sea-colors: the prairie moved in the light like a second-hand sea.

Till between the waters and the wind came the marked-down derelicts with the dollar signs for eyes.

Looking for any prairie portage at all that hadn't yet built a jail.

Beside any old secondhand sea.

14

The portage's single hotel was a barracks, its streets were pig-wallows, and all the long summer night the Pottawattomies mourned beside that river: down in the barracks the horse-dealers and horse-stealers were making a night of it again. Whiskey-and-vermilion hustlers, painting the night vermilion.

In the Indian grass the Indians listened: they too had lived by night.

And heard, in the uproar in the hotel, the first sounds of a city that was to live by night after the wilderness had passed. A city that was to roll boulevards down out of pig-wallows and roll its dark river uphill.

That was to forge, out of steel and blood-red neon, it own peculiar wilderness.

Yankee and *voyageur*, the Irish and the Dutch, Indian traders and Indian agents, halfbreed and quarterbreed and no breed at all, in the final counting they were all of a single breed. They all had hustler's blood. And kept the old Sauganash in a hustler's uproar.

They hustled the land, they hustled the Indian, they hustled by night and they hustled by day. They hustled guns and furs and peltries, grog and the blood-red whiskey-dye; they hustled with dice or a deck or a derringer. And decided the Indians were wasting every good hustler's time.

Slept till noon and scolded the Indians for being lazy.

Paid the Pottawottomies off in cash in the cool of the Indian evening: and had the cash back to the dime by the break of the Indian dawn.

They'd do anything under the sun except work for a living, and we remember them reverently, with Balaban and Katz, under such subtitles as "Founding Fathers," "Dauntless Pioneers" or "Far-Visioned Conquerors."

Meaning merely they were out to make a fast buck off whoever was standing nearest.

They never conquered as well as they hustled—

their arithmetic was sharper than their hunting knives. They skinned the redskin down to his final feather, the forests down to the ultimate leaf of autumn, the farmer out of his last wormy kernel of Indian corn; and passed the rain-swept seasons between cheerfully skinning one another.

One such easy skinner listing his vocation lightly, in the city's first directory, as *Generous Sport*.

Mountain grog seller and river gambler, Generous Sport and border jackal, blackleg braggart and coonskin roisterer, Long Knives from Kentucky and hatchet-men from New York, bondsmen, brokers and bounty jumpers—right from the go it was a broker's town and the brokers run it yet.

It's still the easiest joint in the country in which to jump bond, as well as for staying out of jail altogether. The price commonly being whatever you have in your wallet. If the wallet is empty a fifty-cent cigar will usually do it.

Indeed, the city's very first jailbird got a pass from the city fathers. An antique stray named Harper was knocked down, under the local vagrancy laws, to George White, the Negro town crier, for a quarter. And legally led away by White at the end of a rusty chain.

When antislavery feeling forced the Negro to let the white escape, George wanted only his two

17

bits back. And couldn't collect a dime. So each night scandalized the darkness by crying his loss instead of the hour. He never got his two bits back, but he made a hundred-dollar uproar over it. Every hour on the hour. All night long.

The joint is still in an uproar. Every hour on the hour. All night long.

When the Do-Gooders try to quiet it down they only add drums to the tumult. The village squares arrived too late for a firm toehold.

In 1835 they declared a "season of prayer" and wrested two outlaws right out of the devil's clutches —yet the devil seemed not to miss the pair at all. So they tossed two harder customers into pokey.

And still nobody cared.

Then they fined a brothel-keeper twenty-five silver dollars, and the battle between the Pure-of-Heart and the Brokers' Breed was joined for keeps. The ceaseless, city-wide, century-long guerrilla warfare between the Do-As-I-Sayers and the Live-and-Let-Livers was on. With the brokers breaking in front.

Broke in front and stayed in front despite being crowded to the rail on occasion.

Not that there's been any lack of honest men and women sweating out Jane Addams' hopes here—but they get only two outs to the inning while the

18

hustlers are taking four. When Big Bill Thompson put in the fix for Capone he tied the town to the rackets for keeps.

So that when the reform mayor who followed him attempted to enforce the Prohibition laws, he wakened such warfare on the streets that the Do-Gooders themselves put Thompson back at the wheel, realizing that henceforward nobody but an outlaw could maintain a semblance of law and order on the common highway. Big Bill greeted his fellow citizens correctly then with a cheery, "Fellow hoodlums!"

The best any mayor can do with the city since is just to keep it in repair.

Yet the Do-Gooders still go doggedly forward, making the hustlers struggle for their gold week in and week out, year after year, once or twice a decade tossing an unholy fright into the boys. And since it's a ninth-inning town, the ball game never being over till the last man is out, it remains Jane Addams' town as well as Big Bill's. The ball game isn't over yet.

But it's a rigged ball game.

Once upon a time, when Thirty-fifth Street was the far Southside and North Avenue was the limit on the north, something called the Law-and-Order

19

League shut the Sunday beer halls, and the Beer-on-Sunday Party won the subsequent elections in a walk. A horde of horrified Ohio spinsters thereupon counterattacking the halls by praying at the bar rails, pleading with the drinkers to kneel beside them.

There is no record of anyone getting sawdust in his cuffs: this was 1873, and thousands who had come to rebuild the ruins of the great fire were carrying ragged banners crying BREAD OR BLOOD on the streets. Sunday was the one day of the week the working stiff who was still working had to himself. So he just dipped his kisser deeper into his stein, wiped his moustache tidily and ordered another. He knew he wasn't getting any eight-hour day by kneeling for it.

Indignantly then in their hundreds the women marched to City Hall to demand legal prohibition of Sunday beer—and got turned down there cold. Working stiffs and out-of-work stiffs alike booing them gently back to Ohio.

After times had picked up again a Reverend Gipsy Smith, dressed like midnight itself, led twelve thousand black-gowned and black-tied saviors, carrying flaring torches and half stepping in funeral-march tempo to the menacing *boom* of a single drum, up and down the midnight streets of the old Levee.

The piano rolls stopped on a single surprised chord, the little red lamps blinked out together, the big drum called "Come to Jesus or Else," and the saviors cried in one all-accusing voice, "Where is my wandering boy tonight?"

"He ain't in here, Reverend," some awe-struck sinner answered earnestly—and the little red lamps flickered with laughter, a piano roll lightly tinkled a jeer, and the revelry crashed like window-glass with one deep-purple roar.

And roared on all night long.

"We have struck a blow for Jesus," the reverend announced without changing his shirt.

"A church and a W.C.T.U. never growed a big town yet," Old Cap Streeter contradicted him flatly. "Hit's still a frontier town."

Where the gouging and the cunning and the no-holds-barred spirit of the Middle Border still holds as true as rent day.

For despite the Girl Scouts and the Boy Scouts, the missionary societies and the Bible institutes, the Legion of Decency and Lieutenant Fulmer, Preston Bradley and the Epworth League, Emile Coué and Dwight L. Moody, there's no true season for salvation here. Good times or hard, it's still an infidel's capital six days a week.

And with a driving vigor and a reckless energy

unmatched in the memory of man. Where only yesterday the pungent odor of stewed dog trailed across the marshes, now the million-candled billboards, weaving drunken lights in the river's depths, boast of Old Fitzgerald, Vat 69, White Horse and Four Roses. Where only yesterday the evening crow crossed only lonely tepee fires, now the slender arclamps burn.

To reveal our backstreets to the indifferent stars.

two

are you
a christian?

It's still an outlaw's capital—but of an outlawry whose colors, once crimson as the old Sauganash whiskey-dye, have been washed down, by many prairie rains, to the colorless grey of the self-made executive type playing the percentages from the inside. Under a pale fluorescent glow.

We've abandoned the neighborliness of the Middle Border while sharpening its competitiveness—to lend it a bloodier, more legal edge than the Middle Border ever knew.

For in the time that Dwight L. Moody went about these streets straight-arming strangers with the simple and terrible question, "Are you a Christian?" the answer was simpler and less terrible than now.

Certainly the thief calling himself John the Baptist wasn't one even though he left a religious tract at the scene of every theft. Even though wearing the ministerial black with the Come-to-Jesus-or-Else collar. For he also wore a bright red bandanna about his dirty throat and never a shirt below or beneath at all.

Either you were or you weren't. John the Baptist wasn't one and the bumboat pirate called Black Jack Yattaw wasn't one either. Nor was Paddy the Bear nor Cooney the Fox nor Duffy the Goat.

Nor Red Jimmy Fitzgerald, who conned Charles Francis Adams out of $7,000, and Hungry Joe Lewis, who took Oscar Wilde for another small fortune in that same unchristian year.

Nor Speckled Jimmy Calwell nor Saffo the Greek nor Jew Kid Grabiner. Nor Fancy Tom O'Brien, the King of the Bunko Men; for he murdered Reed Waddell, the inventor of the gold-brick fraud.

Nor the little monster named Mickey Finn, who openly advertised the horror he had devised for the simple pleasure it afforded him to hear some curious innocent order it with his own lips—just before being spun off the stool and into the alley behind the bar. To wake up with the cats looking at him. If he wakened again in the great world at all.

But the Mick was the last of the true infidels.

By the time Hinky Dink Kenna came along you had to cut in closer to answer the reverend's question. For in The Hink the border apache became a working citizen, a property owner assuming civic responsibilities, commanding a ward-wide loyalty and professing some sort of faith or other come Sunday morning. A hustler's hustler, part philanthropist and part straight brigand, The Hink sought his personal salvation in the ballot box.

Like the city that bred him, he had a heavenly harpist on his bedpost as well as a hustler's imp stoking the furnace: when hard times came he fed and sheltered more hungry and homeless men than all the Gold Coast archangels put together. And felt frankly outraged when the archangels accused him of trading free lunches for votes at his Workingman's Exchange.

He'd paid fifty cents in cold cash for every vote he'd bought, he let the archangels know—but what about the missions that were buying blackened souls in exchange for blacker coffee and the easy promise of a heavenly throne? Why was it less noble to pay cash here and now? Let the Gold Coast archangels answer him *that*.

Those same pious Gold Coasters who took the Righteous Horrors at the nightly carnival put on by the First Ward cribs—while secretly pocketing rents off those same terrible cribs.

Yet in standardizing the price of the vote The Hink did more to keep the city running one bitter winter than did all the balmy summers of Moody's evangelism. Not even to mention Lucy Page Gaston's command that the Chicago Cubs stop smoking cigarettes immediately.

Who came out the truer Christian in a hassle like *that*?

For always our villains have hearts of gold and all our heroes are slightly tainted. It always takes somebody like The Hink, in whom avarice and generosity mingled like the hot rum and the cold water in his own Tom-and-Jerries, to run a city wherein warmth of heart and a freezing greed beat, like the blood and the breath, as one.

Somebody like The Hink's Bathhouse John calling on the city, in the name of its little children, to ban the sale of the deadly coffin nail from within two hundred yards of every schoolhouse. Thus earning himself, a buccaneer to his balbriggan underwear, the sanctimonious applause of the *Tribune:*

> By this measure he will drive from the school areas the petty peddlers in death who have been inviting the children to ruin.

Applause which The Bath acknowledged grandly, bowing first to the left and then to the right, in a wondrous tailcoat of billiard-cloth green, lavender trousers, pink gloves and a cream-colored vest flaring with diamonds—to the greatest rogues' circus ever pitched under a single tent.

For all his strutting piety in Lucy Page Gaston's name didn't stop him for one moment from leading his harlots and hopheads, his coneroos and fancymen, his dips and hipsters and heavy-hipted madams—his "willing hands and honest hearts" as he

termed them—to flaunt their soiled banners at the
Annual First Ward Ball.

Out of their dens and out of their dives, out of
their traps and curtained parlors—most of them
carefully masked—The Bath led his willing hands
and honest hearts with his victory over the tobacco
trust in his pocket. And, in the other, plans for a
private zoo. What did his take from the cribs have
to do with whose little children anyhow, The Bath
would have just liked to know.

The fact being that The Hink and The Bath were
the first of the big-time operators. Both living on to
see their territory taken over by the business tweeds
who put a stop to free lunches as being unbusiness-
like.

The Hink and The Bath being the first to suspect
that appeals to Civic Loyalty were appeals to empty
air: that the place had grown up too fast to be con-
scious of itself as a unified city requiring any loyalty
beyond that to the American dollar. "The cult of
money which one encounters here does not spring
from avarice or meanness," one European observer
put it quaintly, "but making money is the only aim
one can set oneself in a city wherein the dollar is the
spiritual denominator as well as the financial one."
The Buck alone lending purpose to the lives of the
anonymous thousands living in anonymous rows

along anonymous streets, under an anonymous moon.

And singing the old crossroads hymns of Faith Everlasting can't help any more, for you can't call anonymous souls to the Lord. He doesn't know who they are.

And the Lord Himself couldn't get some of them that far out into the light anyhow. They'd think Here Comes That Tuesday Night Lineup Again.

You can live your whole life out somewhere between Goose Island and Bronzeville without once feeling that, the week after you move, the neighbors are going to miss your place. For it isn't so much a city as it is a vasty way station where three and a half million bipeds swarm with the single cry, "One side or a leg off, I'm gettin' mine!" It's every man for himself in this hired air.

Yet once you've come to be part of this particular patch, you'll never love another. Like loving a woman with a broken nose, you may well find lovelier lovelies. But never a lovely so real.

Jane Addams too knew that Chicago's blood was hustler's blood. Knowing that Chicago, like John the Baptist and Bathhouse John, like Billy Sunday and Big Bill, forever keeps two faces, one for win-

30

ners and one for losers; one for hustlers and one for squares.

One for the open-eyed children of the thousand-windowed office buildings. And one for the shuttered hours.

One for the sunlit traffic's noontime bustle. And one for midnight subway watches when stations swing past like ferris wheels of light, yet leave the moving window wet with rain or tears.

One face for Go-Getters and one for Go-Get-It-Yerselfers. One for poets and one for promoters. One for the good boy and one for the bad.

One for white collars as well as blue, for our museums like cathedrals and our cathedrals like museums, for the windy white-and-blue miles of our beaches, the Saturday night moonlight excursions to Michigan City, the afternoon at the zoo washed into mists of sunlit remembrance by a sudden warm, still rain; and for that night-shaded honkytonk where Sherry Our Shivering Sheba shook the long night's last weary shake to twenty empty tables and one middle-aged pimp wheedling a deaf bartender for a final double shot.

One for early risers, one for evening hiders.

One for the White Sox and none for the Cubs.

One for King Oliver and Louie Armstrong improvising half an hour on end at the old Lincoln

Gardens Bandstand, for Baby Dodds and Dave Tough and all the other real-gone senders, sent-for-and-gone too soon, who brought jazz up the river from New Orleans, made it Chicago's music and then the world's.

For the soldiers and the sailors and the far-from-home marines, who'll tell you, no matter where you're from, that it's the most open-handed town in the country for any far-from-home soldier.

As well as for old soaks' goat's nests, backstreet brothels, unlit alleys and basement bars: for tavern, trap and tenement. For all the poolroom tigers in checkered caps who've never seen a cow, and all the night-club kittens who've never seen a cloud.

For white-lit showups, dim-lit lockups and the half-lit hallway bedrooms, where the air, along with the bed, is stirred only by the passing of the Jackson Park Express. For all our white-walled asylums and all our dark-walled courtrooms, overheated district stations and disinfected charity wards, where the sunlight is always soiled and there are no holiday hours.

For hospitals, brothels, prisons and such hells, where patronage comes up softly, like a flower.

For all the collarless wanderers of the horse-and-wagon alleys of home.

It isn't hard to love a town for its greater and its

lesser towers, its pleasant parks or its flashing ballet. Or for its broad and bending boulevards, where the continuous headlights follow, one dark driver after the next, one swift car after another, all night, all night and all night. But you never truly love it till you can love its alleys too. Where the bright and morning faces of old familiar friends now wear the anxious midnight eyes of strangers a long way from home.

A midnight bounded by the bright carnival of the boulevards and the dark girders of the El.

Where once the marshland came to flower.

Where once the deer came down to water.

Wheeling around the loop of the lake, coming at Chicago from east and south, the land by night lies under a battle-colored sky. Above the half-muffled beat of the monstrous forges between Gary and East Chicago, the ceaseless signal-fires of the great refineries wave an all-night alarm.

Until, moving with the breaking light, we touch the green pennant of the morning boulevards running the dark-blue boundary of the lake. Where the fortress-like towers of The Loop guard the welter of industrial towns that were once a prairie portage.

It remains a midland portage. No railroad passes through the city. Passengers shift from one to another of half a dozen stations. Freight trains are shunted around belt lines. But the Constellations overhead begin to lend it the look of a mid-world portage, with all the sky for its ocean-port.

The city divided by the river is further divided by racial and lingual differences. The Near Northside, centering around the comical old humpty-dumpty water tower which survived the fire, is, for example, almost as different from the Near Northwest Side, just over the bridge, in manners, mores, vocations and habits of speech, as Bronzeville is from Rogers Park.

So if you're entirely square yourself, bypass the forest of furnished rooms behind The Loop and stay on the Outer Drive till you swing through Lincoln Park. Then move, with the lake still on your square right hand, into those suburbs where the lawns are always wide, the sky is always smokeless, the trees are forever leafy, the churches are always tidy, gardens are always landscaped, streets are freshly swept, homes are pictures out of *Town and Country*. And the people are stuffed with kapok.

For the beat of the city's enormous heart, at the forge in the forest behind the towers, is unheard out in this spiritual Sahara. Where the homes so complacent, and the churches so smug, leave an airlessness like a microscopic dust over the immaculate

34

pews and the self-important bookshelves. The narrow streets of the tenements seem to breathe more easily, as though closer to actual earth, than do these sinless avenues. Where *Reader's Digest* is a faith, the Reverend Bradley is a prophet, and nothing but Sunday morning services can dissuade the hunter one moment from the prey.

three

the
silver-colored
yesterday

All that long-ago August day the sun lay like shellac on the streets, but toward evening a weary small breeze wandered out of some saloon or other, toured Cottage Grove idly awhile, then turned, aimlessly as ever, west down Seventy-first.

The year was 1919, Shoeless Joe Jackson was out-hitting Ty Cobb, God was in his Heaven, Carl Wanderer was still a war hero, John Dillinger was an Indiana farm boy and the cops were looking cautiously, in all the wrong corners, for Terrible Tommy O'Connor.

And every Saturday evening the kid called Nephew and I hauled a little red wagon load of

something called the *Saturday Evening Blade,* a rag
if there ever was one, down Cottage Grove to the
wrought-iron Oakwoods Cemetery gate. There to
hawk it past the long-moldering graves of Confederate prisoners who had died at Camp Douglas
in some long-ago wrought-iron war.

When we sold out we'd just hang around the gate
waiting for Nephew's Uncle Johnson to break out
of the saloon directly across the way. The bartender
ran us off if we came near the doors without the
iron-clad alibi of having a fight to watch, and
Uncle J. was the white hope of that corner.

If no brawl developed of itself the barflies were

certain to arrange something for poor Johnson, an oversized spastic with a puss like a forsaken moose, whose sole idea in battle was to keep his hands in front of his eyes. Some white hope.

Uncle's whole trouble, Nephew confided in me as half owner of the little red wagon, was that he had gone to work too young.

Some uncle. We used to hear him hymning at the bar—

> Oh he walks wit' me
> 'N he talks wit' me—

and the barflies encouraging him mockingly.

He was deeply religious, and the barflies encouraged him in everything—drinking, hymning or fighting, fornication or prayer. As though there were something wondrously comical about everything Uncle attempted.

I remember that poor hatless holy Johnson yet, lurching upon some unsaved little tough with a face shadowed by a cap and a lit cigarette on his lip— the cigarette bobbles and Uncle reels back, blood from his nose coming into his mouth. The Cap yanks him forward, feints his hands down off his eyes and raps him a smashing banneger in the teeth. "It's a case of a good little man whippin' a good big man, that's all," Nephew advised me confidentially, holding our little red wagon behind him. Then the soft shuffle-shuffle of The Cap's shoes imitating the White City professionals.

"Finish the clown off," Nephew encourages The Cap softly. That's the kind of family it was.

Uncle had never learned to fall down. He'd reel, lurch, bleed, bellow and bawl until the bartender would break the thing up at last, wiping Uncle's ashen face with a bar towel in the arc-lamp's ashen light. Till the others came crowding with congratulations right out of the bottle, pouring both into Uncle right there on the street. Then a spot of color would touch his cheeks and he'd break out into that terrible lament—

'N he tells me I am his own.

to show us all he'd won again. Uncle had some such spiritual triumph every Saturday night.

I used to hang open-mouthed around that sort of thing, coming away at last feeling nothing save some sort of city-wide sorrow. Like something had finally gone terribly wrong between the cross atop St. Columbanus and that wrought-iron gate, out of an old wrought-iron war, forever guarding the doubly-dead behind us.

No one could tell me just what.

The wisest thing to do was simply to go beer-cork

hunting behind the saloon. With the city spreading all about. Like some great diseased toadstool under a sheltering, widespread sky. Then to haul our little red wagon slowly home, with Nephew humming all to himself, "Be my little bay-bee bum-bul bee, buzz buzz buzz."

Maybe the whole town went to work too young.

For it's still a Godforsaken spastic, a cerebral-palsy natural among cities, clutching at the unbalanced air: topheavy, bleeding and blind. Under a toadstool-colored sky.

Maybe we all went to work too young.

Yet that was a time of several treasures: one sun-bright-yellow beer cork with a blood-red owl engraved upon it, a Louisville slugger bat autographed by Swede Risberg, and a Comiskey Park program from one hot and magic Sunday afternoon when Nephew and I hid under the cool bleachers for three hours before game time. To come out blinking at last into the roaring stands, with the striped sun on them. And Eddie Cicotte shutting out Carl Mays.

The morning we moved from the far Southside to North Troy Street I had all three treasures on me. And Troy Street led, like all Northside streets— and alleys too—directly to the alien bleachers of Wrigley Field.

"Who's yer fayvrut player?" the sprouts in baseball caps waiting in front of the house had to know before I could pass. I put the horn of the Edison victrola I was carrying down on the sidewalk at my feet before replying. It didn't sound like something asked lightly.

But the suddenly far-distant White Sox had had a competent sort of athlete at short and I considered myself something of a prospect in that position too. "Swede Risberg," I answered confidently, leaning on the Louisville slugger with the autograph turned too casually toward the local loyalty board.

I didn't look like such a hot prospect to North Troy Street, I could tell that much right there and then. "It got to be a National Leaguer," the chairman advised me quietly. So that's how the wind was blowing.

I spent three days leaning on that autograph, watching the other sprouts play ball. They didn't even use American League bats. "Charley Hollocher then," I finally capitulated, naming the finest fielding shortstop in the National League, "account I t'row righty too."

"Hollocher belongs to Knifey," I was informed— but I could fight Knifey for him, I had the right.

I wouldn't have fought Knifey's baby sister for Grover Cleveland Alexander and Bill Killefer thrown in. And could only think nostalgically of the good simple life of the far Southside, where kids had names like "Nephew" and "Cousin," and where a man's place among men could be established by the number of *Saturday Evening Blades* he sold. I went through the entire roster of National League shortstops before finding one unclaimed by anyone else on Troy Street—Ivan Olson, an ex-American Leaguer coming to the end of his career with the team then known as the Brooklyn Robins.

But Olson was taking a lot of booing from the Flatbush crowd that season because he had a habit of protesting a called third strike by throwing his bat in the air—and every time he did it an umpire would pick it up and toss it higher. No eleven-year-old wants to be on the side of any player who isn't a hero to the stands. "If I *got* to pick a Swede"—I stood up to The Committee at last—"I'll stick to Risberg—I seen him play once is why."

Well, you could say your old man was a millionaire if that was your mood and nobody would bother to make you take it back. You might even hint that you knew more about girls than you were telling and still get by. But there wasn't one of those Troy Street wonders who'd yet seen his "fayvrut player" actually play. You had to back that sort of statement up. I pulled out the Comiskey Park program hurriedly.

44

They handed it around in a circle, hand to grubby hand, examining the penciled score for fraud. When it came back to my own hand I was in.

In without selling out: I'd kept the faith with The Swede.

The reason I never got to play anything but right field the rest of that summer I attribute to National League politics pure and simple.

Right field was a coal-shed roof with an American League sun suspended directly overhead. A height from which I regarded with quiet scorn the worshipers of false gods hitting scratchy little National League bloopers far below. There wasn't one honest-to-God American League line drive all summer.

It wasn't till a single sunless morning of early Indian summer that all my own gods proved me false: Risberg, Cicotte, Jackson, Weaver, Felsch, Gandil, Lefty Williams and a utility infielder whose name escapes me—wasn't it McMillen? The Black Sox were the Reds of that October and mine was the guilt of association.

And the charge was conspiracy.

Benedict Arnolds! Betrayers of American Boyhood, not to mention American Girlhood and American Womanhood and American Hoodhood. Every bleacher has-been, newspaper mediocrity and pulpit inanity seized the chance to regain his lost pride at the expense of seven of the finest athletes who ever hit into a double play. And now stood stripped to the bleacher winds in the very sight of Comiskey and God.

I was the eighth. I climbed down from right field to find The Committee waiting.

"Let's see that score card again."

I brought it forth, yellow now with a summer of sun and honest sweat, but still legible. When it came back this time I was only allowed to touch one corner, where a grubby finger indicated the date in July of 1920. Risberg had sold out in the preceding September and I was coming around Troy Street almost a year later pretending I believed Risberg to be an honest man. I'd gone out to the ball park, seen him play in person and was now insisting I'd seen nothing wrong, nothing wrong at all. The moving finger stopped on Risberg's sorrowful name: four times at bat without a hit, caught sleeping off second, and a wild peg to first. And I still pretended I hadn't suspected a *thing?*

"I wasn't there when he *really* thrun the game," I tried to hedge. "It was a different day when he played bum on purpose."

The Tobey of *that* committee was a sprout who had a paying thing going, for weekdays, in the

46

resale of colored paper-picture strips of major-league players. He bought them ten for a penny and resold them to us for two, making himself as high as a dollar a week, of which fifty cents went to his Sunday-school collection plate. I'd once seen his lips moving at the plate, praying for a hit. "What do *you* think he was doin' tossin' wild to first?" this one wanted to know now.

"I figure he was excited, it was a real close play."

"You mean for your all-time All-American fayvrut player you pick a guy who gets excited on the close ones?"

"I didn't know it was for all time," was all I could think to reply. "I thought it was just for this year."

"What kind of American *are* you anyhow?" he wanted to know. He had me. I didn't know what kind I was.

"No wonder you're always in right field where nothin' ever comes—nobody could trust you in center." He was really cutting me up, this crusader.

"Well, I asked for Hollocher in the first place," I recalled.

"You could still fight Knifey for him."

"I'll just take Ivan Olson."

"That's not the question."

"What *is* the question?"

"The question is who was the guy, he knock down two perfec' pegs to the plate in a world-series game, one wit' the hand 'n one wit' the glove?"

"Cicotte done *that*."

" 'N who was Cicotte's roommate?"

Too late I saw where the trap lay: Risberg. I was dead.

"We all make mistakes, fellas," I broke at last. "We all goof off, we're all human—it's what *I* done, I goofed off too—it just goes to show you guys I'm human too. I ain't mad at you guys, you're all good guys, don't be mad at *me*." Choked with guilt and penitence, crawling on all fours like a Hollywood matinee idol, I pleaded to be allowed, with all my grievous faults, to go along with the gang. "Can I still have Olson, fellas? Can I keep my job if I bum-rap some people for you?"

Out of the welter of accusations, half denials and sudden silences a single fact drifted down: that Shoeless Joe Jackson couldn't play bad baseball even if he were trying to. He hit .375 that series and played errorless ball, doing everything a major-leaguer could to win. Nearing sixty today, he could probably still outhit anything now wearing a National League uniform.

Only, I hadn't picked Shoeless Joe. I'd picked the man who, with Eddie Cicotte, bore the heaviest

48

burden of all our dirty Southside guilt. The Black Sox had played scapegoat for Rothstein and I'd played the goat for The Swede.

So wound up that melancholy season grateful to own the fast-fading Olson. When he went back to Rochester or somewhere they started calling me "Olson" too. Meaning I ought to go back to Rochester too. I took that. But when they began calling me "Svenska" that was too much. I fought.

And got the prettiest trimming you'd ever care to see. Senator Tobey himself administered it, to ringing applause, his Sunday-school change jingling righteously with his footwork. Leaving me at last with two chipped teeth, an orchid-colored shiner and no heart left, even for right field, for days.

However do senators get so close to God? How is it that front-office men never conspire? That matinee idols feel such guilt? Or that winners never pitch in a bill toward the price of their victory?

I traded off the Risberg bat, so languid had I become, for a softball model autographed only by Klee Brothers, who were giving such bats away with every suit of boy's clothing bought on the second floor. And flipped the program from that hot and magic Sunday when Cicotte was shutting out everybody forever, and a triumphant right-hander's wind had blown all the score cards across home plate, into the Troy Street gutter.

I guess that was one way of learning what Hustlertown, sooner or later, teaches all its sandlot sprouts. "Everybody's out for The Buck. Even big-leaguers."

Even Swede Risberg.

four

love
is
for barflies

Before you earn the right to rap any sort of joint, you have to love it a little while. You have to belong to Chicago like a crosstown transfer out of the Armitage Avenue barns first; and you can't rap it then just because you've been crosstown.

Yet if you've tried New York for size and put in a stint in Paris, lived long enough in New Orleans to get the feel of the docks and belonged to old Marseille awhile, if the streets of Naples have warmed you and those of London have chilled you, if you've seen the terrible green-grey African light moving low over the Sahara or even passed hurriedly through Cincinnati—then Chicago is your boy at last and you can say it and make it stick:

That it's a backstreet, backslum loudmouth whose challenges go ringing 'round the world like any green punk's around any neighborhood bar where mellower barflies make the allowances of older men: "The punk is just quackin' 'cause his knees is shakin' again."

"What's the percentage?" the punk demands like he really has a right to know. "Who's the fix on this corner?"

A town with many ways of fixing its corners as well as its boulevards, some secret and some wide open. A town of many angry sayings, some loud and some soft; some out of the corner of the mouth and some straight off the shoulder.

"You make rifles," the Hoosier fireman told ten thousand workingmen massed at a Socialist picnic here, "and are always at the wrong end of them."

"Show me an honest man and I'll show you a damned fool," the president of the Junior Steam-fitters' League told the visiting president of the Epworth League.

"I don't believe in Democracy," the clown from the National Association of Real Estate Boards re-assured his fellow clowns. "I think it stinks."

"I'll take all I can get," the blind panhandler added, quietly yet distinctly, in the Madison Street halfway house.

"You can get arrested in Chicago for walking down the street with another man's wife," the cops forewarn the out-of-town hustler smugly.

"I despise your order, your law, your force-propped authority," the twenty-two-year-old defied the ancient remaindered judge. "Hang me for it!"

And the strange question inscribed for posterity on every dark, drawn shade of the many-roomed brothel that once stood on Wells and Monroe, asked simply:

WHY NOT?

"A lot you got to holler," the wardheeler who protected many such drawn shades subsequently advised the crusading minister. "You live off the people down in your patch too, don't you?"

"If you're that smart"—the hustler put a stop to the argument—"why ain't you no millionaire?"

Cruising down Milwaukee Avenue on any Loop-bound trolley on any weekday morning, the straphangers to Success who keep the factories and the ginmills running stand reading the papers that could as well be published in Israel or Athens, in Warsaw or in Rome. On either side of the tracks are the shops with the American signs in one window and alien legends in the other: Spanish, Polish, Italian, Hebrew, Chinese or Greek.

Between stops stretch the streets where the shadow of the tavern and the shadow of the church form a single dark and double-walled dead end. Narrow streets where the summer sun rocks, like a Polish accordion, with a louder, shinier, brassier blare than American music anywhere. Churches that look as though they'd been brought over whole, without a brick missing, from Stockholm and Lodz, Dublin or Budapest: from all the old beloved places. Negro churches, as often as not, bearing Hebrew characters out of some time when the building was a synagogue.

Yet the city keeps no creed, prefers no particular spire, advances no one color, tolerates all colors: the dark faces and the blue-eyed tribes, the sallow Slavs and the olive Italians. All the creeds that persecution harassed out of Europe find sanctuary on this ground, where no racial prejudice is permitted to stand up.

We insist that it go at a fast crawl, the long way around.

The Negro is not seriously confronted here with a stand-up and head-on hatred, but with something psychologically worse: a soft and protean awareness of white superiority everywhere, in everything, the more infuriating because it is as polite as it is impalpable. Nobody even *thought* such a thing, my dear.

So we peg the rents just a teensy-weensy bit— say twenty-five per cent—if you happen to be a Negro and so can well afford it.

If you're black you'd better afford it.

If you're white,

a Forty-seventh Street minstrel sometimes sings, mostly to himself,

Well, awright.
If you're brown, stick aroun'.
If you're black, step back

Step back
Step back
Step back.

And no one will ever name the restaurants you
mustn't eat in nor the bars you mustn't drink at.
Find them out for yourself, greyboy. Make your
own little list. Of the streets you mustn't live on, the
hotels where you can't register, the offices you
can't work in and the unions you can never join.
Make a good long list and have it typed in triplicate.
Send one copy off to Senator Douglas and one to
King Levinsky.

The King and the Senator are equally con-
cerned.

You can belong to New Orleans. You can belong
to Boston or San Francisco. You might conceivably
—however clandestinely—belong to Philadelphia.
But you can't belong to Chicago any more than you
can belong to the flying saucer called Los Angeles.
For it isn't so much a city as it is a drafty hustler's
junction in which to hustle awhile and move on out
of the draft.

That's why the boys and girls grow up and get
out.

Forever fancying some world-city right out of the
books wherein some great common purpose lends

meaning to their lives. As no brokers' portage ever can.

So they go to New York and merely grow sharp. Or they go to Hollywood and soften like custard left in the Sunset Boulevard sun.

Or to Paris, the top of the sky and the end of the world, for the special sort of wonder they cannot live without—and find nothing but American pansies packed three deep at the bars and aging American divorcées in summer furs carting pekes around in baskets especially constructed for the peke trade. When the peke-and-pansy season is past they get one fleeting glint of the City of Light like their world-city out of the books—and know, in that swift homesick moment, that they're as close to home, and as far, as ever they'll be.

For Paris and London and New York and Rome are all of a piece, their tendrils deep in the black loam of the centuries; like so many all-year-round ferns tethered fast in good iron pots and leaning always, as a natural plant ought, toward what little light there is. But Chicago is some sort of mottled offshoot, with trailers only in swamp and shadow, twisting toward twilight rather than to sun; a loosely jointed sport too hardy for any pot. Yet with that strange malarial cast down its stem.

You can be a typical Parisian, you can be a typical

New Yorker if that helps when the cocktail lounges close. But if you can find anything in pants, skirts or a Truman Capote opera cape passing itself off as a typical Chicagoan we'll personally pay his fare back to *Flair*.

New York has taken roots as deep as the Empire State Building is tall. Detroit is a parking lot about a sports arena. New Orleans is mellow where it isn't sear. St. Louis, albeit still green in spots after lo these many springs, has definitely had it. Kansas City has gone as far as it can go. San Francisco is complete. Philadelphia appears finished.

But Hustlertown keeps spreading itself all over the prairie grass, always wider and whiter: the high broken horizon of its towers overlooks this inland sea with more dignity than Athens' and more majesty than Troy's. Yet the caissons below the towers somehow never secure a strong natural grip on the prairie grasses.

A town that can look, in the earliest morning light, like the fanciest all-around job since Babylon. And by that same night, south down State or north on Clark or west on Madison, seem as though the Pottawattomies had been the wisest after all.

Most native of American cities, where the chrome-colored convertible cuts through traffic ahead of the Polish peddler's pushcart. And the long, low-lighted

59

parlor-cars stroke past in a single, even yellow flow. Where the all-night beacon guiding the stratoliners home lights momently, in its vasty sweep, the old-world villages crowding hard one upon the other.

Big-shot town, small-shot town, jet-propelled old-fashioned town, by old-world hands with new-world tools built into a place whose heartbeat carries farther than its shout, whose whispering in the night sounds less hollow than its roistering noontime laugh: they have builded a heavy-shouldered laugher here who went to work too young.

And grew up too arrogant, too gullible, too swift to mockery and too slow to love. So careless and so soon careworn, so challenging yet secretly despairing—how can such a cocksure Johnson of a town catch anybody but a barfly's heart?

Catch the heart and just hold it there with no bar even near?

Yet on nights when, under all the arc-lamps, the little men of the rain come running, you'll know at last that, long long ago, something went wrong between St. Columbanus and North Troy Street. And Chicago divided your heart.

Leaving you loving the joint for keeps.

Yet knowing it never can love you.

five

bright faces
of tomorrow

Giants lived here once. It was the kind of town, thirty years gone, that made big men out of little ones. It was geared for great deeds then, as it is geared for small deeds now.

In Vachel Lindsay's day, in Carl Sandburg's day, in the silver-colored yesterday, in Darrow's and Masters' and Edna Millay's day, writers and working stiffs alike told policemen where to go, the White Sox won the pennant with a team batting average of .228 and the town was full of light.

Now it's the place where we do as we're told, praise poison, bless the F.B.I., yearn wistfully for just one small chance to prove ourselves more abject than anyone yet for expenses to Washington and return—You Too Can Learn to Trap Your Man—and applaud the artist, hanging for sale beside his work, with an ancestral glee. And cannot understand how it can be that others are happier than ourselves. And why it seems that no one loves us now as they once did. No giants live on Rush Street any more.

Since the middle twenties the only party of over-average height to stop off here awhile was a Mississippi Negro named Wright. And he soon abandoned his potentialities, along with his people, somewhere along Forty-seventh Street. Potentialities still lying around behind some chicken shack or other down there, gathering mold about the edges but still too heavy for any one else on Forty-seventh, or anywhere else in town for that matter, to lift. While, rumor has it, he preoccupies himself with the heady task of becoming a Café Flore intellectual. With approximately the same equipment for such a task as Herb Graffis. For the artist lucky enough to come up in Chicago there ought to be a warning engraved on the shinbone alley tenement which was once Wright's home: Tough it out, Jack, tough it out.

"With two exceptions," Mencken observed in 1930, "there is not a single novelist deserving the attention of the civilized reader's notice who has not sprung from the Chicago palatinate."

Out of the Twisted Twenties flowered the promise of Chicago as the homeland and heartland of an American renaissance, a place of poets and sculptors to come, of singers and painters, dancers, actors and actresses of golden decades yet to be. Jane Addams and Bix Beiderbecke and Mary Garden and Billy Petrolle and Grover Cleveland Alexander were working their happy wonders then. Gene Field had gone, but Dreiser and Anderson and Masters and Sandburg were still here.

Thirty years later we stand on the rim of a cultural Sahara with not a camel in sight. The springs dried up and the sands drifted in, and the caravans went the other way. The names of our writers are one with the fighters whose names are legends: Battling Nelson and Barney Ross, Willie Joyce and Tony Zale, Tuffy Griffiths and Miltie Aron, Billy Marquart and Davey Day. Today, whether speaking of writers or fighters or ballplayers, the only true major-leaguers batting hereabouts are all working out of Comiskey Park.

(And what became of No-Hit Charley Robertson, who stepped off a sandlot one afternoon to pitch that perfect game for the White Sox? What ever became of No-Hit Charley, who put twenty-seven men down on strikeouts and infield popups—and then stepped back to his sandlot and left nothing behind but that perfect afternoon when nobody in the world could get a hit?)

And what became of the old Bismarck Gardens, that stood where the Marigold stands now? What became of Sam T. Jack's Burlesque and the old Globe on Desplaines? Who remembers the electrified fountain that was once the showpiece of Lincoln Park? Who now knows the sorrowful long-ago name of the proud steamer *Chicora,* down with all hands in the ice off South Haven? Or where all the high-wheeled open-front hacks went, with the velvet robe in the back and the jack handle in front in case of trouble? Gone with the days when Patrick Henry beer sold for four dollars a quarter barrel and White Swan gin for twenty-nine cents a half pint; gone with Emile Coué, gone with old Sam Insull, gone with Billy Sunday, gone with Great Man Shires. Sunk under the ice in the waves off South Haven, sunk with all hands for good and forever, for keeps and a single day.

The city today is more a soldier's than an artist's town. It has had its big chance, and fluffed it. Thirty years ago we gave musicians to the world; now we give drill sergeants and "professional informants," formerly just "informers."

You can live in a natural home, with pictures on the walls, or you can live in a fort; but it's a lead-pipe cinch you can't live in both. You can't make an arsenal of a nation and yet expect its great cities to produce artists. It's in the nature of the overbraided brass to build walls about the minds of men—as it is in the nature of the arts to tear those dark walls down. Today, under the name of "security," the dark shades are being drawn.

Yet, looking east to the cocktail-lounge culture of New York or west to the drawn shades of Hollywood, where directors go on all-fours begging producers, "Please kick me, it will show the world how deeply I respect you," we can agree complacently with the old wardheeler from Wells and Monroe telling the visiting crusader, "A lot *you* got to holler."

A lot we all got to holler.

"Watch out for yourself" is still the word. "What can I do for you?" still means "What can you do for me?" around these parts—and that's supposed to make this the most American of cities too. It's always been an artist's town and it's always been a torpedo's town, the most artistic characters in the strong-arm industry as well as the world's most muscular poets get that way just by growing up in Chicago—and that's an American sort of arrangement too they tell us.

So whether you're in the local writing racket or in the burglary line, if you're not a bull then you'd better be a fox. Wise up, Jim: it's a joint where the bulls and the foxes live well and the lambs wind up head-down from the hook. On the day that the meek inherit the rest of the earth they'll be lining up here for unemployment insurance and be glad to be getting it.

A town where the artist of class and the swifter-type thief approach their work with the same lofty hope of slipping a fast one over on everybody and making a fast buck to boot. "If he can get away with it I give the man credit," is said here of both bad poets and good safeblowers. Write, paint or steal the town blind—so long as you make your operation pay off you'll count nothing but dividends and hear nothing but cheers. Terrible Tommy O'Connor was never a hero till he walked past the hangman and out the door and never came back any more.

Make the *Tribune* bestseller list and the Friends of American Writers, the Friends of Literature, the Friends of Shakespeare and the Friends of Frank Harris will be tugging at your elbow, tittering down your collar, coyly sneaking an extra olive into your martini or drooling flatly right into your beer with the drollest sort of flattery and the cheapest grade of praise: the grade reserved strictly for proven winners.

But God help you if you're a loser and unproven to boot: the bushytails will stone your very name. "Hit him again, he don't own a dime" is the rock upon which the Gold Coast literati have builded along with the blowsiest North Clark Street tart. "Let's see your dirty gold, Jack," is how you're judged on either The Coast or The Street. "This is a high-class parlor, we ain't doin' business in no gangway, bud."

Therefore its poets pull the town one way while its tycoons' wives pull it another, its gunmen making it the world's crime capital while its educators beat the bushes for saints. Any old saints. And every time a Robert Hutchins or a Robert Morss Lovett pulls it half an inch out of the mud, a Hearst or an Insull or a McCormick shoves it down again by sheer weight of wealth and venality.

Up, down and lurching sidewise—small wonder we're such a Johnson of a joint. Small wonder we've had trouble growing up.

The very toughest sort of town, they'll tell you—*that's* what makes it so American.

Yet it isn't any tougher at heart than the U.S.A. *is* tough at heart, for all her ships at sea. It just acts with the nervous violence of the two-timing bridegroom whose guilt is more than he can bear: the bird who tries to throw his bride off the scent by accusing her of infidelity loudly enough for the neighbors to hear. The guiltier he feels the louder he talks. That's the sort of little loud talker we have in Chicago today. He isn't a tough punk, he's just a scared one. Americans everywhere face gunfire better than guilt.

Making this not only the home park of the big soap-chip and sausage-stuffing tycoons, the home cave of the juke-box giants and the mail-order dragons, the knot that binds the TV waves to the airlanes and the railroad ties to the sea, but also the psychological nerve center where the pang goes deepest when the whole country is grinding its teeth in a nightmare sleep.

Here, where we've kept the frontier habit of the Big Bluff most intact, the hearts of Americans, who must go along with the Big Bluff or be investigated, are most troubled.

Congressman Lincoln once told Polk that he was "like a man on a hot shovel finding no place on which he could sit down," meaning that the torch Polk's brass was putting to another people's fields was not Democracy's torch after all. If he could say a word in Springfield again this morning he might assure us that we've got the wrong shovel again.

Here, where hope was highest, the disappointment digs deepest.

You can't push nineteen-year-olds who want to be good doctors and good engineers into a war for the salvation of importers' investments and expect them to come out believing in anything much beyond the uses of the super-bazooka against "gooks." You can see the boys who stopped caring in 1917 under the city arc-lamps yet.

Under the tall lamps yet. As evening comes taxiing in and the jungle hiders come softly forth: geeks and gargoyles, old blown winoes, sour stewbums and grinning ginsoaks, young dingbats who went ashore on D Plus One or D Plus Two and have been trying to find some arc-lit shore ever since. Strolling with ancient box-car perverts who fought all their wars on the Santa Fe.

Deserters' faces, wearing the very latest G.I. issue: the plastic masks of an icy-cold despair. Where the sick of heart and the lost in spirit stray. From the forgotten battlegrounds on the other side of the billboards, on the other side of the TV commercials, the other side of the headlines. Fresh from the gathering of snipes behind the nearest KEEP OFF warnings come the forward patrols of tomorrow. Every day is D-day under the El.

By highway and by byway, along old rag-tattered walls, surprised while coming up in the grass by the trolley's green-fire flare, their faces reveal, in that ash-green flash, a guilt never their very own.

Upon the backstreets of some postwar tomorrow, when the city is older yet, these too shall live by night.

Bright faces of tomorrow: whiskey-heads and hop-heads, old cokey-joes and musclemen on the prowl for one last wandering square to muscle before the final arc-lamp dims. When the poolrooms all are padlocked and the juke-boxes all are still. When the glasses all are empty. And, under the torn and sagging ties of the long-blasted El, the last survivors cook up the earth's final mulligan. To toast man's

71

earth derisively with the earth's last can of derail: "Let's give it back to the squares."

When traffic no longer picks up, as traffic used to do.

"When it come to Democracy they had to take *our* brand in them days," surviving veterans may recall. "Our brand or else. The goon squads saw to *that*. They went out of business shortly after that." We all went out of business shortly after that.

These are the pavement-colored thousands of the great city's nighttime streets, a separate race with no place to go and the whole long night to kill. And no Good-Morning nor Good-Evening-Dears for the freshly combed tribe of Riders-to-Work-by-Morning nor the dusty-collared clan of Riders-to-Home-by-Dusk.

Tonight, just as the daylight's last sleepy Boy Scout is being tucked in with a kiss and a prayer, the sullen evening's earliest torpedo slips the long cue silently from the shadowy rack. Touches the shaded lamp above the green-baized cloth and turns on the night.

Every day is D-day under the El.

six

no more
giants

It used to be a writer's town and it's always been a fighter's town. For writers and fighters and furtive torpedoes, cat-bandits, baggage thieves, hallway headlockers on the prowl, baby photographers and stylish coneroos, this is the spot that is always most convenient, being so centrally located, for settling ancestral grudges. Whether the power is in a .38, a typewriter ribbon or a pair of six-ouncers, the place has grown great on bone-deep grudges: of writers and fighters and furtive torpedoes.

"City of the big shoulders" was how the white-haired poet put it. Maybe meaning that the shoulders had to get that wide because they had so many bone-deep grudges to settle. The big dark grudge cast by the four standing in white muslin robes, hands cuffed behind, at the gallows' head. For the hope of the eight-hour day.

The grudge between Grover Cleveland and John Peter Altgeld. The long deep grudges still borne for McCormick the Reaper, for Pullman and Pullman's Gary. Grudges like heavy hangovers from men and women whose fathers were not yet born when the bomb was thrown, the court was rigged, and the deed was done.

And maybe it's a poet's town for the same reason it's a working stiff's town, both poet and working stiff being boys out to get even for funny cards dealt by an overpaid houseman weary long years ago.

And maybe it's a working stiff's and a poet's town because it's also an American Legionnaire's town, real Chamber of Commerce territory, the big banker-and-broker's burg, where a softclothes dick with a paunch and no brain at all, simply no brain at all, decides what movies and plays we ought to see and what we mustn't. An arrangement sufficient to make a sensitive burglar as well as a sensitive poet look around for the tools closest to hand.

Town of the hard and bitter strikes and the trigger-happy cops, where any good burglar with a sheet a foot long can buy a pass at a C-note per sheet: half a sheet, half a bill. Two sheets, two bills. Yes, and where the aces will tell the boy behind the bars, "Come on out of there, punk. You ain't doin' us no good in there. Out on the street 'n get it up—everythin' over a C you get to keep for yourself 'n be in court with it at nine tomorrow or we'll pick you up without it 'n fit you for a jacket."

Where undried blood on the pavement and undried blood on the field yet remembers Haymarket and Memorial Day.

Most radical of all American cities: Gene Debs' town, Big Bill Haywood's town, the One-Big-Union town. Where woodworkers once came out on the

First of May wearing pine shavings in their caps, brewers followed still wearing their aprons, and behind them the bakers, the barbers, the cornice-makers, tin-roofers and lumber-shovers, trailed by clerks and salesmen. As well as the town where the race riots of 1919 broke and the place where the professional anti-Semites still set up shop confident of a strong play from the North Shore.

Town of the flagpole sitters, iron city, where everything looks so old yet the people look so young. And the girl who breaks the world's record for being frozen into blocks of ice between sprints at the Coliseum Walkathon breaks the selfsame record every night. And of that adolescent who paused in his gum-chewing, upon hearing the sentence of death by electrocution passed upon him, to remember ever so softly: "Knew I'd never get to be twenny-one anyhow."

Town of the small, cheerful apartments, the beer in the icebox, the pipes in the rack, the children well behaved and the TV well tuned, the armchairs fatly upholstered and the record albums filed: 33 rpm, 45 rpm, 78 rpm. Where the 33 rpm husband and proud father eats all his vitamin-stuffed dinner cautiously and then streaks to the bar across the street to drink himself senseless among strangers, at 78 rpm, all alone.

Town of the great international clowns, where the transcontinental Barnum-and-Bailey buffoons stand on their heads for a picture on the sports page, a round of applause, a wardful of votes, a dividend or a friendly smile: Big Bill Thompson, King Levinsky, Yellow Kid Weil, Gorgeous George, Sewell Avery, Elizabeth Dilling, Joe Beauharnais, Sam Insull, Botsy Connors, Shipwreck Kelly, The Great I Am, and Oliver J. Dragon. And, of course, the Only-One-on-Earth, the inventor of modern warfare, our very own dime-store Napoleon, Colonel McGooseneck.

Town of the classic boners and the All-Time All-American bums, where they score ten runs after two are gone in the last of the ninth when the left-fielder drops an easy popup that should have been the third out. Final score: 10–8. Where somebody is always forgetting to touch second. And the local invincible, the boy most likely to be champion, faints open-eyed on the ropes in the very first round without being struck a blow because the champion is coming right toward him.

"I'll do any damned thing you boys want me to do," Mayor Kelly told his boys gratefully, and he kept his word.

Town of the great Lincolnian liberals, the ones who stuck out their stubborn necks in the ceaseless battle between the rights of Owners and the rights of Man, the stiff-necked wonders who could be broken but couldn't be bent: Dreiser, Altgeld, Debs.

The only town for certain where a Philadelphia first-baseman can answer an attractive brunette's invitation to step into her room: "I have a surprise for you"—and meet a shotgun blast under the heart. "The urge kept nagging at me and the tension built up. I thought killing someone would relieve it." For the sad heart's long remembrance.

Town of the blind and crippled newsies and the pinboys whose eyes you never see at all. Of the Montgomery-Ward sleepwalkers and all the careworn hopers from home with Expressman Death in their eyes reading all about it on the Garfield Park Local.

Town of the topless department stores, floor upon floor upon floor, where a sea-green light from the thousand-globed chandeliers drifts down the scented air, across oriental rugs and along long gleaming glass: where wait the fresh-cut sirloin tips, the great bloody T-bones and the choice center-cut pork chops, all with a freezing disdain for the ground hamburger.

A Jekyll-and-Hyde sort of burg, where one university's faculty members can protest sincerely against restrictive covenants on the blighted streets bordering their campus—not knowing that the local pay roll draws on real estate covered by covenants like a tent. Let's get back to them saints, Professor. It's awful cold out there.

As the carillons of twelve A.M. divide the campus from the slum.

"The slums take their revenge," the white-haired poet warned us thirty-two American League seasons and Lord-Knows-How-Many-Swindles-Ago. "Always somehow or other their retribution can be figured in any community."

The slums take their revenge. And you can take your pick of the avengers among the fast international set at any district-station lockup on any Saturday night. The lockups are always open and there are always new faces. Always someone you never met before, and where they all come from nobody knows and where they'll go from here nobody cares.

The giants cannot come again; all the bright faces of tomorrow are careworn hustlers' faces.

And the place always gets this look of some careworn hustler's tomorrow by night, as the arch of spring is mounted and May turns into June. It is then that the women come out of the summer hotels to sit one stone step above the pavement, surveying the men curb-sitting one step below it. Between them pass the nobodies from nowhere, the nobodies nobody knows, with faces cut from the same cloth as their caps, and the women whose eyes reflect nothing but the pavement.

The nameless, useless nobodies who sleep behind the taverns, who sleep beneath the El. Who sleep in burnt-out busses with the windows freshly curtained; in winterized chicken coops or patched-up truck bodies. The useless, helpless nobodies nobody knows: that go as the snow goes, where the wind blows, there and there and there, down any old cat-and-ashcan alley at all. There, unloved and lost forever, lost and unloved for keeps and a day, there far below the ceaseless flow of TV waves and FM waves, way way down there where no one has yet heard of phonevision nor considered the wonders of techni-color video—there, there below the miles and miles of high-tension wires servicing the miles and miles of low-pressure cookers, there, there where they sleep on someone else's pool table, in someone else's hall or someone else's jail, there where they chop kindling for heat, cook over coal stoves, still burn kerosene for light, there where they sleep the all-night movies through and wait for rain or peace or snow: there, there beats Chicago's heart.

There, unheard by the millions who ride the waves above and sleep, and sleep and dream, night after night after night, loving and well beloved, guarding and well guarded, beats the great city's troubled heart.

And all the stately halls of science, the newest Broadway hit, the endowed museums, the endowed opera, the endowed art galleries, are not for their cold pavement-colored eyes. For the masses who do the city's labor also keep the city's heart. And they think there's something fishy about someone giving them a museum for nothing and free admission on Saturday afternoons.

They sense somebody got a bargain, and they are so right. The city's arts are built upon the uneasy consciences that milked the city of millions on the grain exchange, in traction and utilities and sausage-stuffing and then bought conscience-ease with a minute fraction of the profits. A museum for a traction system, an opera building for a utilities empire. Therefore the arts themselves here, like the acres of Lorado Taft's deadly handiwork, are largely statuary. Mere monuments to the luckier brokers of the past. So the people shy away from their gifts, they're never sure quite why.

The place remains a broker's portage. And an old-time way station for pimps as well. Both professions requiring the same essential hope of something for nothing and a soft-as-goosefeathers way to go. A portage too for the fabulous engines: the Harvester, the sleeping car and the Bessemer Process.

Yet never a harvest in sight hereabouts for humanity's spirit, uprooted over half the world and well deceived here at home.

No room, no time, no breath for the Bessemer processes of the heart.

seven

nobody knows
where
o'connor went

An October sort of city even in spring. With some-body's washing always whipping, in smoky October colors off the third-floor rear by that same wind that drives the yellowing comic strips down all the gut-ters that lead away from home. A hoarse-voiced extry-hawking newsie of a city.

By its padlocked poolrooms and its nightshade neon, by its carbarn Christs punching transfers all night long; by its nuns studying gin-fizz ads in the Englewood Local, you shall know Chicago.

By nights when the yellow salamanders of the El bend all one way and the cold rain runs with the red-lit rain. By the way the city's million wires are burdened only by lightest snow; and the old year yet lighter upon them. When chairs are stacked and glasses are turned and arc-lamps all are dimmed. By days when the wind bangs alley gates ajar and the sun goes by on the wind. By nights when the moon is an only child above the measured thunder of the cars, you may know Chicago's heart at last:

You'll know it's the place built out of Man's ceaseless failure to overcome himself. Out of Man's endless war against himself we build our successes as well as our failures. Making it the city of all cities most like Man himself—loneliest creation of all this very old poor earth.

And Shoeless Joe, who lost his honor and his job, is remembered now more fondly here, when stands are packed and a striped sun burns across them, than old Comiskey, who salvaged his own.

On hot and magic afternoons when only the press box, high overhead, divides the hustler and the square.

For there's a left-hander's wind moving down Thirty-fifth, rolling the summer's last straw kelly across second into center, where fell the winning single of the first winning Comiskey team in thirty-two seasons.

Thirty-two American League seasons (and Lord knows how many swindles ago), Nephew is doing thirty days again for the fifteenth or the thirty-ninth time (this time for defacing private property), nobody knows were O'Connor went and a thousand Happy-Days-Are-Here-Again tunes have come and gone. And the one that keeps coming back softest of all, when tavern lights come on and the night is impaled by the high-tension wires, goes:

> It's only a paper moon
> Hanging over a cardboard sea

For everybody takes care of himself under this paper moon, and the hustlers still handle the cardboard. Joe Felso doesn't trouble his pointy little head just because somebody tossed a rock through some other Joe Felso's window two doors down. It wasn't his window and it wasn't his rock and we all have our own troubles, Jack.

The big town is getting something of Uncle Johnson's fixed look, like that of a fighter working beyond his strength and knowing it. "Laughing even as an ignorant fighter laughs, who has never lost a battle," the white-haired poet wrote before his hair turned white.

But the quality of our laughter has altered since that appraisal, to be replaced by something sounding more like a juke-box running down in a deserted bar. Chicago's laughter has grown metallic, the city no longer laughs easily and well, out of spiritual good health. We seem to have no way of judging either the laughter of the living or the fixed smirk of the dead.

The slums take their revenge. How much did he *have*, is what we demand to know when we hear good old Joe Felso has gone to his reward. Never what *was* he, in human terms. Was his income listed publicly? Was there a Ford in his future at the very moment he was snatched? And whether he was of any use or any joy to himself, when he had his chance for use and joy, we never seem to wonder. It's hustle and bustle from day to day, chicken one day and feathers the next, and nobody knows where O'Connor went.

Nobody will tell how Tommy got free.

Nor whether there are well-springs here for men beneath the rubble of last year's revelry.

The pig-wallows are paved, great Diesels stroke noiselessly past the clamorous tenements of home. The Constellations move, silently and all unseen, through blowing seas above the roofs. Only the measured clatter of the empty cars, where pass the northbound and the southbound Els, comes curving down the constant boundaries of night.

The cemetery that yet keeps the Confederate dead is bounded by the same tracks that run past Stephen A. Douglas' remains. The jail where Parsons hung is gone, and the building from which Bonfield marched is no more. Nobody remembers the Globe on Desplaines, and only a lonely shaft remembers the four who died, no one ever understood fully why. And those who went down with the proud steamer *Chicora* are one with those who went down on the *Eastland*. And those who sang "My God, How the Money Rolls In" are one with those who sang, "Brother, Can You Spare a Dime?"

And never once, on any midnight whatsoever, will you take off from here without a pang. Without forever feeling something priceless is being left behind in the forest of furnished rooms, lost forever down below, beneath the miles and miles of lights and lights. With the slow smoke blowing compassionately across them like smoke across the spectrum of the heart. As smoky rainbows dreaming, and fading as they dream, across those big fancy Southside jukes forever inviting you to put another nickel in, put another nickel in whether the music is playing or not.

As the afternoon's earliest juke-box beats out rumors of the Bronzeville night.

A rumor of neon flowers, bleeding all night long, along those tracks where endless locals pass.

Leaving us empty-handed every hour on the hour.

Remembering nights, when the moon was a buffalo moon, that the narrow plains between the billboards were touched by an Indian wind. Littered with tin cans and dark with smoldering rubble, an Indian wind yet finds, between the shadowed canyons of The Loop, patches of prairie to touch and pass.

Between the curved steel of the El and the nearest Clark Street hockshop, between the penny arcade and the shooting gallery, between the basement gin-mill and the biggest juke in Bronzeville, the prairie is caught for keeps at last. Yet on nights when the blood-red neon of the tavern legends tether the arc-lamps to all the puddles left from last night's rain, somewhere between the bright carnival of the boulevards and the dark girders of the El, ever so far and ever so faintly between the still grasses and the moving waters, clear as a cat's cry on a midnight wind, the Pottawattomies mourn in the river reeds once more.

The Pottawattomies were much too square. They left nothing behind but their dirty river.

While we shall leave, for remembrance, one rusty iron heart.

The city's rusty heart, that holds both the hustler and the square.

Takes them both and holds them there.

For keeps and a single day.